MW00452808

Boy Returning
Water to the Sea
Koans for Kelly Fearing

Andrea Selch

Cockeyed Press
Chapel Hill, North Carolina

Text copyright © 2009 Andrea Selch
Images copyright © 1948, 1949, 1955, 1963, 1964, 1968,
1973, 1974, 1978, 1982, 1985, 1993 William Kelly Fearing,
and are reprinted here by special arrangement with the artist.

All rights reserved. No part of this book may be reproduced
in any form or by electronic or mechanical means, including
information storage and retrieval systems, without written
permission of the publisher, except by reviewers who may
quote brief passages in reviews.

Published in 2009 by Cockeyed Press, Chapel Hill, NC 27515
www.cockeyedpress.com

Design: Anita Mills

ISBN-978-0-9790623-0-8

Cover Image:
Boy Returning Water to the Sea, by William Kelly Fearing, © 1949.

For Kelly Fearing in his nintieth year...

Man Doing Isolation, Horseback

1948, Conte Conte on Cameo paper

"Come," say the muscles, as the man
reaches up, "come uncover youth."
Beneath him, his mare grazes onward,
onward, into Tantric old age.

The cameo paper is filled
with the noise of a thousand birds.

Man doing Isolation, horseback   Kelly Fearing   May 1980

Boy Returning Water to the Sea

1949, Oil on Canvas

Yes, there's a need for it—every
azure splash, proto-icicle, -iceberg, -teardrop,
-steamcloud rising from a stormdrain,
-rusty puddle just stepped in.

Boys will be boys, but then also men:

His mantle is tattered, his feet torn,
and the handles of the basket are gone.

The Place of Tobias and the Angel

1955, Oil on canvas

For fish gall for his father's eyes, Tobias
lowers his line. It's light, but the drop
is plumb—only a hook, and hope, for bait.

      His father's eyes—once bright hazel, able
      to discern spun warp, felt weft—now cloudy
      as winter sky, the muddied Euphrates.

      The winter sky, above the Tigris,
      is rife with birds—Crested Larks, Sand Martins,
      a single Lesser Kestrel heading south.

      Birds crowd the shore as well, hunting
      under the scrub pine. What do they know
      of sons, of fathers, the curses their droppings stir?

On a cliff above him, the angel Rafe
also hopes, as angels do, though
with his wings pinned back—impeccable.

Poet and Bird before an Open Cave

1963, Oil on canvas

Even though it's a fantasy,
they don't speak
the same language.
The man hears "Squawk, squawk."
The bird wonders what interest
there is in a bush,
albeit a fragrant one
like Rosemary.

But through the cave
another sky is visible.

Little Pink-Faced Owl with Butterflies

1964, Oil crayon, gold and silverleaf, collage on Color-aid paper

On a background of blue and gold
with one butterfly below, one above,
the owl's interest is in the distance:
mouse, vole, horizon where the sun's long gone.

Then through the forest canopy the rain comes
pouring—like acid wash, erasure of certainty—
and the brown and the green are one,
and the lattice of sticks (the nest) is undone.
Whatever was gold is gone; though after the clouds,
the moon rises: waxing gibbous, fleet, fine.

In the gold there was copper; in the blue, fuschia;
and in the butterflies, flecks of the fallen sun's last rays.
Little pink-faced owl, if she could choose otherwise,
she'd still choose butterflies.

The Night of the Rhinoceros

1968, Oil on Canvas

Why should he wait for morning?
He is light on his three toes, beguiling,
striped with wrinkles, wrinkles, wrinkles,
and pointed at hock, hip, horns.
Above him, in cobalt-becoming-marine,
the four swallows follow;
wherever he's going will be home.

Owl with the Secret of the Enneagram

1968, Acrylic and gold leaf on linen

"There are secrets and then there are secrets,"
says the owl born in the Year of the Rooster
only it sounds like *hoo hoo, hoo hoo*
and the blue linen behind him wrinkles in jest.

"Shall I dance for you with my one wing
under two orange suns, counting steps
three, four, five, six, seven,
or back off angrily, screeching,

"'The secret is number one'?"

Holy Shell Waiting for the Return of the Soul
(Homage to Hugo van der Goes), Shell Collage No. 7

1973, Collage, opals and acrylic

The Difficult Toy

1948, Casein on linen

For when the mother went to bury her boy,
she held him thus, under the arms
for when the boy was a baby
she held him under the arms, facing the ocean
for if the joy of the child
could make her forget the pain of childbirth
for when he was crowning, she felt
his skull, like a shell, yet soft
(for when my son came, he came facing backward)
for when the shell came from the ocean
it held the sound of the waves
for the ear that heard the ocean in the shell
for the ear that heard only the ocean
for when the boy was a baby
we held him
thus

for the boy who saw in the ocean his mother
for when Hugo painted him
his eyes were open
for Hugo painted his eyes closed
for when Hugo let his paintbrush fall
for when he wept

for the shell waiting on its boy
for the shell the painter found
for painting it engendered
for when he's painting he's in the ocean
for if the shell had fallen from his hands

for when he grew within her like a Volute or Olive
at first armless

for when the paintbrush fell from his hands
for Hugo's headache—a crown of thorns—and he closed his eyes
for when his own death would be a relief, the release of a breath too long held
for when Hugo dropped his brush at the sea
for when the mother holds her son
limp in her arms
for sadness like a stab in the gut
for blood that poured from the wound like an afterbirth
for the shell that waits
holding the ocean inside it
to be returned to the waters
to tumble again in the tide's polishing chamber

for Hugo limp in his studio chair, his arms at his sides
for the paintbrush he could no longer clutch
for the painters whose work carries forth their predecessors
like aging fathers
for the ocean which is mother to painting
for painting which is the father of poetry

for the ocean which swept in
tumbling shells like a great polishing chamber
for the shells it polished
for the mother whose child grew without arms
for the boy who, rather than paint, would pose like a crow,
head down, on his arms
for the boy not a boy any longer
speaking of laying down arms
for the boy with no father
for whose son was Hugo?
for my son, crow-boy, whom I've snatched
from the ocean under the arms a dozen times
for the boy who played with shells at the beach,
who named them, Volute, Olive, Baby's Ear, King's Crown, Sunray Venus, Angel Wings
for when he's playing he's in the ocean

Come boy, come. Let go of your difficult toy
for the painter has dropped his brush
at the lip of the sea

The Zebra's Secret is Silver

1974, Oil on canvas

It is important to begin at the beginning—
not Aardvark or Antelope, but Aquamarine—
and not to trouble yourself, at first,
about composition, just listen
to shadow and mist, the fan of whiskers
from a muzzle not quite black.
Everyone and every thing has already come,
already gone, so there's no hurry:
Without hoof prints behind or before him,
the Zebra stands on a small green hill
flicking his bristly tail—"No."

Two Giraffes in Arizona

1978, Oil on canvas

In this view, she still seems to be following him,
as she has been 29 years,
from the zoo, through their escape,
and now in the raspberry desert, where
their great necks no longer qualify them fittest—
the cactus's sumptuous flesh
is beyond their reach.

But she has stopped, lop-eared, frowning:
Why couldn't it be *one going one way,
the other, the other*? Why?

Texas is Much Smaller Here Floating through the Equinox
Collage with Street Transformation No. 3

1982, Found objects and opals

What he'll miss isn't the sky, uninterrupted by trees,
or the tumbleweeds tumbling like cartoons of themselves,
not the hills, where there are hills, nor the fenceposts,
uncountable, punctuating the road. Not the heat in the summer,
nor the rain, when it rains, nor the way winter
lets you see miles away in perfect focus.
Not the drawl, which he doesn't notice anymore,
nor the tea always sweet. Not the light
nor the darkness. Not the difficult poses, passages,
transcendence, when he has managed them. Not the gratitude,
returns or restrikes. But the debris—rust and opals—
that can be made, so easily, to speak.

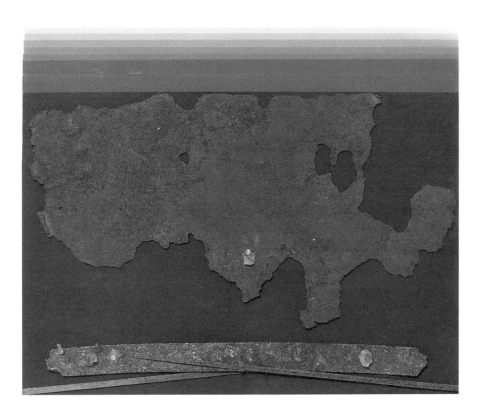

Large Bird Listening to the Sounds of Purple

1976-85, Colored pencil

Nine years he stood, neck curved,
wings not quite folded down,
until what he heard
announced its hue—
not violet, lilac, amethyst,
but colored-pencil purple.

To the eye, it's nearly red.

Then close your eyes.

Watching Lightning #24

1993, Collage, Prismacolor pencil

Three pink fish are enough,
among the fingers of seaweed,
to suggest more.

Though the lightning is still very far off,
its tentacles have already shattered
the lavender sky.

So be it.

List of Illustrations

Man Doing Isolation, Horseback, William Kelly Fearing, 1948, Conté crayon on white Cameo paper, 11-3/4 in. x 9 in.

Boy Returning Water to the Sea, William Kelly Fearing, 1949, Oil on canvas, 16 in. x 20 in.

The Place of Tobias and the Angel, William Kelly Fearing, 1955, Oil on canvas, 40 in. x 30 in.

Poet and Bird Before an Open Cave, William Kelly Fearing, 1963, Oil on canvas, 36 in. x 30 in.

Little Pink-Faced Owl with Butterflies, William Kelly Fearing, 1964, Oil crayon with gold and silver leaf and collage on Color-aid paper, 18 in. x 9 in.

The Night of the Rhinoceros, William Kelly Fearing, 1968, Oil on canvas, 40 in. x 30 in.

Owl with the Secret of the Enneagram, William Kelly Fearing, 1968, Acrylic and gold leaf on linen, 16 in. x 12 in.

Holy Shell Waiting for the Return of the Soul (Homage to Hugo van der Goes) Shell Collage No. 7, William Kelly Fearing, 1973, Collage, opals, and acrylic, 10 in. x 8 in.

The Difficult Toy, William Kelly Fearing, 1948, Casein on linen, 13-7/8 in. x 8 in.

The Zebra's Secret is Silver, William Kelly Fearing, 1974, Oil on canvas, 30 in. x 40 in.

Two Giraffes in Arizona, William Kelly Fearing, 1978, Oil on canvas, 20 in. x 16 in.

Texas is Much Smaller Here Floating through the Equinox: Collage with Street Transformation No. 3, William Kelly Fearing, 1982, Found objects and opals, 7-1/4 in. x 8-3/4 in.

Large Bird Listening to the Sounds of Purple, William Kelly Fearing, 1976-85, Prismacolor Pencil, 12-3/4 in. x 16 in.

Watching Lightning #24, William Kelly Fearing, 1993, Prismacolor pencil, collage, 8 in. x 9 in.

Andrea Selch was born in New York City in 1964 and moved to North Carolina in 1983. She has an MFA from UNC-Greensboro, and a PhD from Duke University, where she taught creative writing from 1999 until 2003. Her poems have been published in *Calyx*, *Equinox*, *The Greensboro Review*, *Oyster Boy Review*, *Luna*, *The MacGuffin*, and *Prairie Schooner*. Her poetry chapbook, *Succory*, was published by Carolina Wren Press in 2000. Her full-length collection *Startling* was originally published by Turning Point Press in 2004, after placing in the 2003 Turning Point competition, and was reissued by Cockeyed Press in 2009. In 2001, she joined the board of Carolina Wren Press and is now its President and Executive Director. She lives in rural Hillsborough with her partner and their two children.

Photo of Andrea Selch by Diane Amato.

William Kelly Fearing, painter, printmaker and educator, was born in Arkansas in 1918. He received his BA from Louisiana Polytechnic Institute in 1941 and his MA from Teachers College, Columbia University, in 1950. He is Ashbel Smith Professor of Art Emeritus at the University of Texas, Austin, where he taught from 1947 until 1987. A former member of the Fort Worth Circle, his work has been widely exhibited and collected by individuals, galleries and institutions such as the El Paso Museum of Art, Gallery of Visual Arts of Louisiana Tech, Fort Worth Art Center, Witte Memorial Museum, Marion Koogler McNay Art Museum, Carnegie Institute, Pennsylvania Academy of Art, Houston Museum of Fine Arts, Dallas Museum of Fine Art, Denver Art Museum, and the Philbrook Art Center, among many others.

In 2002, the U.T. Department of Art and Art History presented a 60-year retrospective of his work, entitled *The Mystical World of Kelly Fearing*. That exhibit brought together paintings, drawings, prints and collages from public and private collections throughout the United States and also traveled to The University of Texas at Arlington and the Old Jail Art Museum in Albany, Texas.

In 2007, Fearing was the recipient of the E. William Doty Award, established in 1995 by the U.T. College of Fine Arts. It is the highest recognition given to individuals of distinction in their fields, and/or those who have demonstrated extraordinary interest in the college.

Photo of Kelly Fearing by Rebecca McEntee,
© Austin American-Statesman/WPN, 2002.